T5-CQF-072

On Love
and other Essays
with some Aphorisms

A. R. ORAGE
ON LOVE

WITH SOME APHORISMS
& OTHER ESSAYS

SAMUEL WEISER
734 Broadway
New York
1974

DISCARD

UNITY SCHOOL LIBRARY
UNITY VILLAGE, MISSOURI 64065

First American Paperback Edition 1974
By Samuel Weiser, Inc.

© Janus Press

All rights reserved. This book, or
parts thereof, must not be reproduced
in any form without prior permission
from the publisher.

ISBN: 0-87728-264-1
Library of Congress Catalog Card Number: 78-17779

DISCARD

Printed in U.S.A. by
NOBLE OFFSET PRINTERS, INC.
NEW YORK, N.Y. 10003

CONTENTS

ON LOVE

FREELY ADAPTED FROM THE TIBETAN

YOU must learn to distinguish among at least three kinds of love (though there are seven in all): instinctive love, emotional love, and conscious love. There is not much fear that you cannot learn the first two, but the third is rare and depends upon effort as well as intelligence. Instinctive love has chemistry as its base. All biology is chemistry, or perhaps we should say alchemistry; and the affinities of instinctive love, manifesting in the attractions, repulsions, mechanical and chemical combinations we call love, courtship, marriage, children and family, are only the human equivalents of a chemist's laboratory. But who is the chemist here? We call it Nature. But who is Nature? As little do we suspect as the camphor which is married to the banyan suspects a gardener. Yet there is a gardener. Instinctive love, being chemical, is as strong, and lasts as long, as the substances and qualities of which it is the manifestation. . . . These can be known and measured only by one who understands the alchemical progression we call heredity. Many have remarked that happy or unhappy marriages are hereditary. So, too, are the number of children, their sex, longevity, etc. The so-called science of astrology is only the science (when it is) of heredity over long periods.

Emotional love is not rooted in biology. It is, in fact, as often anti-biological in its character and direction.

7

Instinctive love obeys the laws of biology, that is to say, chemistry, and proceeds by affinities. But emotional love is often the mutual attraction of disaffinities and biological incongruities. Emotional love, when not accompanied by instinctive love (as it seldom is), rarely results in offspring; and when it does, biology is not served. Strange creatures arise from the embraces of emotional love, mermen and mermaids, Bluebeards and des belles dames sans merci. Emotional love is not only short-lived, but it evokes its slayer. Such love creates hate in its object, if hatred is not already there. The emotional lover soon becomes an object of indifference and quickly thereafter of hatred. These are the tragedies of love emotional.

Conscious love rarely obtains between humans; but it can be illustrated in the relations of man to his favourites in the animal and vegetable kingdoms. The development of the horse and the dog from their original state of nature; the cultivation of flowers and fruit—these are examples of a *primitive* form of conscious love, primitive because the motive is still egoistic and utilitarian. In short, Man has a personal use for the domesticated horse and the cultivated fruit; and his labour upon them cannot be said to be for love alone. The conscious love motive, in its developed state, is the wish that the object should arrive at its own native perfection, regardless of the consequences to the lover. 'So she become perfectly herself, what matter I?' says the conscious lover. 'I will go to hell if only she may go to heaven'. And the paradox of the attitude is that such

8

love always evokes a similar attitude in its object. Conscious love begets conscious love. It is rare among humans because, in the first place, the vast majority are children who look to be loved but not to love; secondly, because perfection is seldom conceived as the proper end of human love—though it alone distinguishes adult human from infantile and animal love; thirdly, because humans do not know, even if they wish, what is good for those they love; and fourthly, because it never occurs by chance, but must be the subject of resolve, effort, self-conscious choice. As little as Bushido or the Order of Chivalry grew up accidentally does conscious love arise by nature. As these were works of art, so must conscious love be a work of art. Such a lover enrols himself, goes through his apprenticeship, and perhaps one day attains to mastery. He perfects himself in order that he may purely wish and aid the perfection of his beloved.

Would one enrol in this service of conscious love? Let him forswear personal desire and preconception. He contemplates his beloved. What manner of woman (or man) is she (or he)? A mystery is here: a scent of perfection the nascent air of which is adorable. How may this perfection be actualized—to the glory of the beloved and of God her Creator? Let him think, is he fit? He can only conclude that he is not. Who cannot cultivate flowers, or properly treat dogs and horses, how shall he learn to reveal the perfection still seedling in the beloved? Humility is necessary, and then deliberate tolerance. If I am not sure what is proper to her

9

perfection, let her at least have free way to follow her own bent. Meanwhile to study—what she is, and may become; what she needs, what her soul craves and cannot find a name, still less a thing, for. To anticipate today her needs of tomorrow. And without a thought all the while of what her needs may mean to me. You will see, sons and daughters, what self-discipline and self-education are demanded here. Enter these enchanted woods, ye who dare. The gods love each other consciously. Conscious lovers become gods.

Without shame people will boast that they have loved, do love or hope to love. As if love were enough, or could cover any multitude of sins. But love, as we have seen, when it is not conscious love—that is to say, love that aims to be both wise and able in the service of its object—is either an affinity or a dis-affinity, and in both cases equally unconscious, that is, uncontrolled. To be in such a state of love is to be dangerous either to oneself or to the other or to both. We are then polarized to a natural force (which has its own objects to serve regardless of ours) and charged with its force; and events are fortunate if we do not damage somebody in consequence of carrying dynamite carelessly. Love without knowledge and power is demoniac. Without knowledge it may destroy the beloved. Who has not seen many a beloved made wretched and ill by her or his 'lover'? Without power the lover must become wretched, since he cannot do for his beloved what he wishes and knows to be for her delight. Men should pray to be spared the experience of love without wisdom and strength. Or, finding themselves in love, they should pray for knowledge and power to guide their love. Love is *not* enough.

'I love you', said the man. 'Strange that I feel none the better for it', said the woman.

The truth about love is shown in the order in which religion has been introduced into the world. First came the religion of Power, then came the religion of Knowledge, and last came the religion of Love. Why this order? Because Love without the former qualities is dangerous. But this is not to say that the succession has been anything more than discretion: since Power alone, like Knowledge alone, is only less dangerous than Love alone. Perfection demands simultaneity in place of succession. The order is only evidence that since succession was imperative (man being subject to the dimension of Time which is succession), it was better to begin with the less dangerous dictators and leave Love to the last. A certain prudent man, when he felt himself to be in love, hung a little bell round his neck to caution women that he was dangerous. Unfortunately for themselves they took too much notice of it; and he suffered accordingly.

Until you have wisdom and power equal to your love, be ashamed, my sons and daughters, to avow that you are in love. Or, since you cannot conceal it, love humbly and study to be wise and strong. Aim to be worthy to be in love.

All true lovers are invulnerable to everybody but their beloved. This comes about not by wish or effort but by the fact of true, i.e. whole, love alone. Temptation has not to be overcome: it is not experienced. The invulnerability is magical. Moreover, it occurs more often than is usually supposed. Because 'unfaithfulness' is manifested, the conclusion is drawn that invulnerability does not exist. But 'infidelity' is not necessarily due to temptation, but possibly and often to indifference; and there is no Fall where there is no Temptation. Men should learn to discriminate in themselves and in women real and assumed invulnerability. The latter, however eloquent, is due to fear. Only the former is the fruit of love. Another prudent man, desiring, as all men and women do in their hearts, invulnerability in himself and in the woman he loved, set about it in the following way. He tasted of many women and urged his beloved to taste of many men. After a few years he was satisfied that nothing now could tempt him. She, on the other hand, had had no doubt of herself from the beginning. She had been born invulnerable; he had attained it.

The state of being in love is not always defined in relation to one object. One person has the talisman of raising another to the plane of love (that is, of polarizing him or her with the natural energy of love); but he or she may not be then either the sole beloved or, indeed, the beloved at all. There are, among people as among chemical substances, agents of catalysis which make possible interchanges and combinations into which the catalysts themselves do not enter. Frequently they are unrecognized by the parties affected, and usually by themselves as well. In the village of Bor-na, not far from Lhassa, there once lived a man who was such a catalyst.

12

People who spoke to him instantly fell in love, but not with him, or, indeed, immediately with anybody in particular. All that they were aware of was that they had, after conversation with him, an active spirit of love which was ready to pour itself out in loving service. The European troubadours were perhaps such people.

There is no necessary relation between love and children; but there is a necessary relation between love and creation. Love is for creation; and if creation is not possible, then for procreation; and if even that is not possible, then for creations of which, perhaps fortunately, we are unconscious. Take it, however, as the fundamental truth about Love: that it always creates. Love created the world: and not all its works are beautiful! The procreation of children is the particular function of instinctive love: that is its plane. But above and below this plane, other kinds of love have other functions. Emotional love is usually instinctive love out of place; and its procreations are in consequence misfits in the world. The higher forms of love, on the other hand, either exclude procreation, not artificially but naturally, or include it only as a by-product. Neither the purpose nor the function of conscious love is children; unless we take the word in the mystic sense of becoming as little children. For briefly, the aim of conscious love is to bring about rebirth, or spiritual childhood. Everbody with perceptions beyond those of male and female must be aware of the change that comes over the man or woman, however old in years, who loves. It is usually instinctive; yet it symbolizes the still more marvellous change oc-

13

curring when a man or woman loves consciously or is aware of being consciously loved. The youth in such cases has all the air of eternity; and it is, indeed, the divine youth. The creations of such a spiritual child in each of the two lovers is the peculiar function of conscious love; and it depends neither upon marriage nor upon children. There are other creations proper to still higher degrees of love; but they must remain until we have become as little children.

We are not one but three in one; and the fact is represented in our physiological make-up. The three main systems, cerebral, nervous, and instinctive, exist side by side, sometimes appearing to co-operate, but more often failing, and usually at cross-purposes. In relation to the external world it depends upon the system in charge of the organism at the moment what the response to any given stimulus will be. If the cerebral system is on duty —that is temporarily in charge of the organism—the response will be one. If the nervous or instinctive system is alone awake, the replies will be different. Three quite different people, each with his own ideas of how his organism should act, exist in us at once: and usually they refuse to co-operate with each other, and, in fact, get in each other's way. Now imagine such an organism, tenanted by three squabbling persons, to 'fall in love'. *What* has fallen in love; or, rather, which of the three? It seldom happens that all three are in love at the same time or with the same object. One is in love, the others are not; and either they resist, or, when the lover is off guard, make his organism unfaithful (driving the poor lover to lies and deceit or self-reproach); or they are forced into submission, battered into acquiescence. In such circumstances, which every candid reader will recognize, what is a lover?

You imagine that you are continent because you have refrained from sex-relations; but continence is of the senses as well as of the organs, and of the eyes chiefly. From each of the senses there streams energy—energy as various as the man himself. It is not only possible but it is certain that we can expend ourselves intellectually, emotionally or sexually through any one of the senses. To look with lust is much more than simply to look: it is to expend one of the finer substances of which complete sex-energy is composed: something passes in the act of vision which is irrecoverable; and for the want of it the subsequent sex-life is incomplete. It is the same with the other senses, though less easily realized. In short, it is possible to become completely impotent by means of the senses alone—yes, by the eyes alone— while remaining continent in the ordinary meaning of the word.

The chastity of the senses is natural in a few people; but by the many it must be acquired if it is to become common. Under the greatest civilization human history has yet known, the capital of which was the city whose poor remains are Bagdad, the chastity of the senses was taught from early childhood. Each sense was carefully trained; and exercises were devised to enable pupils to discriminate the different emanations arriving from the sense perceptions intellectually, emotionally, instinct-

15

ively or erotically motived. From this education people acquired the power of directing their senses, with the result that chastity was at least possible, since it was under control. Eroticism thereby became an art, in the highest form the world has seen. Its faint echoes are to be found in Persian and Sufi literature today.

Bluebeard and La Belle Dame are the male and female types respectively of the same psychology—inspirers of hopeless because unrequitable passion. The decapitated ladies who hung about Bluebeard's chamber were really about his neck; and they had only to let go to be free. Similarly the pale warriors and princes in the cave of La Belle Dame were there by choice, if an irresistible attraction can be called choice. The legends present Bluebeard and La Belle Dame from the point of view of their escaped victims, that is to say, as monsters delighting in erotic sacrifice. But both were as much victims as their titular victims; and both suffered as much, if not more. In such cases of uncontrolled attraction, power passes through the medium, who thus becomes formidably magnetic; and men and women in sympathetic relation are drawn towards him or her like filings towards a magnet. At first, no doubt, the experiences of a Bluebeard or La Belle Dame are pleasant and fortifying to self-pride and self-vanity. The other sex is at their feet. But when, having realized that the power is neither their own nor under their control, they discover that they too are victims, the early satisfaction is dearly paid for. The cure for all parties is difficult. It consists in the re-education of the body and the senses.

Love without divination is elementary. To be in love demands that the lover shall divine the wishes of the beloved long before they have come into the beloved's own consciousness. He knows her better than she knows herself; and loves her more than she loves herself; so that she becomes her perfect self without her own conscious effort. *Her* conscious effort, when the love is mutual, is for him. Thus each delightfully works perfection in the other.

But this state is not ordinarily attained in nature: it is the fruit of art, of self-training. All people desire it, even the most cynical; but since it seldom occurs by chance, and nobody has published the key to its creation, the vast majority doubt even its possibility. Nevertheless it is possible, provided that the parties can learn and teach humbly. How to begin? Let the lover when he is about to see his beloved think what he should take, do, or say so as to give her a delightful surprise. At first it will probably be a surprise that is not a complete surprise: that is to say, she will have been aware of her wish, and only delighted that her lover had guessed it. Later the delightful surprise may really surprise her; and her remark will be: 'How did you know I should be pleased, since I should never have guessed it myself?' Constant efforts to anticipate the nascent wishes of the beloved while they are still unconscious are the means to conscious love.

Take hold tightly; let go lightly. This is one of the great secrets of felicity in love. For every Romeo and Juliet tragedy arising from the external circumstances of the two parties, a thousand tragedies arise from the circumstances created by the lovers themselves. As they seldom know the moment or the way to 'take hold' of each other, so they even more rarely know the way or the moment to let go. The ravines of Mount Meru (i.e. Venusberg) are filled with lovers who cannot leave each other. Each wishes to let go, but the other will not permit it. There are various explanations of this unhappy state of affairs. In most instances the approach has been wrong: that is to say, the parties have leapt into union without thought of the way out. Often the first five minutes of the lovers' *first* meeting are decisive of the whole future of the relations. In some instances the original relation has been responsible for the subsequent difficulty of 'letting go': it should never have been; or not have been in the precise circumstances of its occurrence. Mistimed relations always cause trouble. In other cases the difficulty is due to difference in age, education, or 'past'. One is afraid to 'let go' because it appears to be the last hope, or because too much time has already been spent on it, or because it has been the best up to date, or because his 'ideal', created by education, demands eternal fidelity even where it is not possible, because it is not desired by both; or because one is over-sensitive from past experience and cannot face another failure, or because the flesh being willing the spirit is weak, i.e. neither party can use a knife; or because circumstances are unfavourable, i.e. the parties must continue to see each other; or because of imagination, as when one or the other pictures the happiness of the other without him or her. There are a thousand explanations, and every one of them, while sufficient as a cause, is quite inadequate as reason, the fact being that when one of the parties desires to separate, the other's love-duty is to 'let go'. Great love can both let go and take hold.

Jealousy is the dragon in paradise; the hell of heaven; and the most bitter of the emotions because associated with the sweetest. There is a specific against jealousy, namely, conscious love; but this remedy is harder to find than the disease is to endure. But there are palliatives of which the first therapeutic condition is the recognition of the disease and the second the wish to cure oneself. In these circumstances let the sufferer deliberately experiment. Much may be forgiven him or her during this process. He may, for instance, try to forward the new plans of his former beloved—but this is difficult without obvious hypocrisy. Or he may plunge into new society. Or he may engage himself in a new work that demands all his energy. Or he may cast a spell on his memory and regard his former beloved as dead; or as having become his sister; or as having gone away on a long journey; or as having become enchanted. Best, however, if he 'let go' completely with no lingering hope of ever meeting her again.

Be comforted. Our life is but one day of our Life. If not today, tomorrow! Let go!

ON RELIGION

Suppose that a remote posterity, unversed in mathematics and the scientific research equipment of our age, should inherit one of our current science manuals. There they would read, or rather, decipher, such statements as that light travels at the rate of 186,000 miles a second; that the sun is 92,000,000 miles distant from the earth and that the light of the nearest star takes four and a half light years to reach us. What would they make of it all? Some of them, it is probable, would hold that their forerunners must have possessed a faculty lost to themselves, and in consequence would attach a mystical significance to the unverifiable dogmas; they might even repeat these dogmas as possibly magical formulas. But undoubtedly the best common sense of the day, in the absence of the means, or any conception of the means, of verification, would dismiss the statements as being childish guesses or, at best, as barbarous abracadabra. Only a very few would suspect that perhaps we were not such fools as we appeared, and give us suspended credit for a method behind our madness. But our method itself and the instruments we employ would be still to seek.

The foregoing picture may serve to illustrate what may possibly—let us say no more than possibly—be our very own situation in regard to the ancient 'science' of religion. We have inherited a few of the text-books once circulated among the illuminati of more or less extinct civilizations, and we find them to contain statements of equal exactitude and incredibility concerning things of which we have no verifiable knowledge, as that there is a God Who is a trinity of Persons, Who created the Universe according to Reason, and Man in His own image, and Who placed us in the world with potentialities of consciously becoming like unto Himself. Some of us to-day are disposed, like our imagined descendants, to take these traditional statements mystically; to repeat them as magical formulas; and to assume that a lost faculty, the so-called religious sense, was possessed by our ancestors of ancient Egypt, India, Persia and Syria. So relatively powerful, in fact, are these that their attitude towards the inherited dogmas of ancient religion is still the standard of respectability. The weight of common sense, however, is slowly but surely making itself felt; and the day is not far off when the intelligence of our civilization will explicitly decline even to be interested in grandiose statements apparently insusceptible of proof. Only a few, a very few, will continue to suspect that perhaps the Egyptians, the Buddhists, the Pythagoreans and the Gnostics were people very like ourselves in respect of faculty and unlike us in the same respect in which we shall differ from a remote posterity without our science, namely, in the possession, not of a lost faculty, but of a lost method or technique. And for these few, too, the method or technique is still to seek—or perchance only to recognize.

Let us assume that we belong to these few and that we begin, at least roughly, to define the conditions essential to our hopeful quest of the lost technique. The first, obviously, is the discrimination of Religion from the subjects with which it has been associated in the course of time. As certainly as our descendants would, if they were so much interested, at least give our Science the distinction of being concerned about some definite field of possible or, maybe, impossible knowledge, and discriminate between our Science and our Ethics, our Science and our Sociology, our Science and our popular customs, so we undoubtedly can at once begin to distinguish in the traditional religion of our ancient forerunners certain characteristics unique and peculiar to the subject. Whether verifiable or not, whether even intelligible to us or not, it is clear that the statements concerning Religion contained in the surviving texts assume certain specific generalizations as to the World and Man and, either as cause or as effect, certain specific attitudes and rational obligations laid upon Man himself. Still roughly, they can be said to be as follows: that the Universe is an intelligent and therefore intelligible Cosmos; that the obligation and, at the same time, the highest possible aim of Man is to understand and to co-operate with the intelligent laws that govern it; that in order to accomplish this a special way of life or technique is necessary; and that this technique consists primarily in a method of 'divinizing', that is to say, of raising to a higher conscious level Man's present state of being. Everything essential, it seems, to an elementary definition of Religion, as the subject has come down to us, is contained in this brief summary. There is the cosmological element, for instance, missing from our Sociology and Ethics. The cosmology, moreover, differs from the cosmology of our Science in assuming universal pyschological values; everything is God, and therefore intelligent and potentially intelligible to Reason. Man has a unique and designed place and, therefore, function, in the cosmological scheme. In other words, he enters into obligations by being born. At the same time, his awareness of his place and function is not a gift of nature: he must acquire it by a special effort and by a special method. Finally, both his development and his own greatest happiness depend upon his discovery of his function and his conscious discharge of it.

This outline is formidable enough to daunt the rational seeker after the rationale of ancient Religion. Without prepossessions for or against these specific dogmas of our forefathers, but with, nevertheless, a benevolent curiosity as to the possible method involved in them, how are we even to begin our search? Certainly there is little in modern science, or in any branch of it, to provide us with even a hint of a method of verification. Of any means of knowing if an intelligent God exists, our Science is completely and indifferently ignorant; and naturally and consequently all the lesser branches of knowledge, springing from the same trunk, must equally dispense with the hypothesis of God's existence. Equally, too, our current working conceptions must dispense with unproven potentialities such as are assumed in the religious statements concerning Man's possible conscious divinization by understanding, becoming and service. What may be may equally not be; and our Science deals only with potentialities actualised, neither with Reality nor

23

with Potentiality metaphysically, but with Actuality, that is to say, the physical. No exception can be made either in the case of Philosophy or in the case of Psychology. Both are too good pupils of the scientific school to resist for long the full employment of the actualistic method. There linger, it is true, medieval ghosts in both fields who speculate hither and thither in the hope of finding pasture for their souls, but with the increasing chemicalization of psychology, everything dependent upon psychological processes, such, for instance, as speculative philosophy, will more and more lose scientific value, as being insufficiently radical. Sooner or later, the question in regard to every philosophical or psychological opinion will be not its value as an objective statement but its value as merely a symptom of personal chemistry.

With no sure guide in the religious traditions themselves and with not the least glimmer of light from modern Science, our quest for the possible or not impossible technique employed by our ancestors in formulating their 'dogmas' seems doomed on the threshold of failure. And rationally it must be so. If we cannot accept on faith the doctrines and assumptions specifically associated with Religion, nor can find in modern Science even the end of a clue that promises to reveal it to us, our case is lost from the beginning. And we must reconcile ourselves with Science as we have it and remember only as an ancient dream the faith of our forefathers. By the same token, our dreams of the future must similarly be shepherded through the Gates of Horn. For, with the admission that we neither have discovered nor can begin

24

to discover the yet not impossible technique of religion as formulated by our ancestors, we must deny ourselves the scientific hope of discovery in the future. If modern Science can throw no light on the Religion of the past —on Religion, that is to say, as defined above—neither can it promise us a Religion in the future.

The field of Religion, chimerical or not, can no more be changed than the field of any other department of Science, actual or so-called. Religion, like Ethics or Physics, is, by definition, what it is and always will be. And by declining to be so much as interested in the question of a technique of Religion, Science declares itself bankrupt of Religion for ever.

Things, however, are seldom as black as rationalism paints them; and scientists fortunately are not all as scientific as their science. In short, there are loopholes of escape from our impasse; and one of the most promising is to be found in modern psychology; precisely, in fact, in the latest conquest of the scientific method, the field of Behaviourism. Behaviourism, there is no doubt, has come to stay. It is true that Behaviourism is still in little more than the elementary stage, that we have still much to learn and certainly some surprising discoveries to anticipate; but the method that has begun to collect and verify the data of human pyschology at its source, that is to say, in observable behaviour beginning with earliest infancy, is assuredly destined to supersede the psuedo-scientific methods of introspection and psycho-analysis. Henceforward for Science there is only one possible approach to psychology, the approach of observation, verification and experiment. Every other approach is now medieval.

The question, however, is what and whose behaviour we are to observe; or, without prejudice to any other field, the legitimacy of a field of observation which, as we have said, on the face of it appears to promise some light on our inquiry concerning a technique of Religion. To be explicit, is self-observation, together with the unusual sequel in the scientific method—verification, hypothesis, experiment and demonstration—equally legitimate with the observation of others; and, if it is, can we devise a method to ensure its rigorous pursuit? Are we ourselves, as behaving organisms, a valid subject for our scientific research—assuming, of course, that we employ the same objective means as we should employ in the case of others? Is self-knowledge at least as possible scientifically as the knowledge of anything else? There can be no doubt of the reply; and Behaviourists, in fact, have admitted it. Though, at the outset, self-observation as a scientific method of research into human psychology labours under both acquired and natural disabilities, as, for example, association with introspection and the presence of the personal equation in its most intimate form, neither its past nor its inherent difficulty can reasonably be said to disqualify it. All that would be necessary would be to be doubly on guard against subjectivity and to be all the more rigorously and objectively scientific in sight of the snares of misunderstanding and self-deception.

That self-observation has at least an affinity with the

26

subject-matter of Religion is obvious by inspection. A characteristic of Religion is concern with oneself next to God. On closer examination, indeed, this self-concern in every possible sense proves to be one of the leading motives and fundamental suppositions of Religion as it has come down to us. The poignancy of religious phraseology concerning the lot and fate of Man, the hopes and fears of his salvation, the speculations concerning the nature of the individual soul, the promises of divinization, all indicate self-concern not merely instinctive but visceral and cerebral. The individual in Religion is mightily concerned for himself but for himself in every possible and even impossible way. Everything he does, including not only his acts but his thoughts and feelings, may be and, from the point of view of Religion, is held to be, at least potentially, profoundly significant. The individual's awareness of and concern for himself in the highest possible degree is assumed as one of the very conditions of the religious life.

We may conclude, therefore, that if self-awareness, or, let us say, self-consciousness, is not the sole or main aim of Religion as formulated in our texts, at least it is an implied pre-requisite of the main aim which appears to be the understanding and service of the Creator, God. All the commandments, injunctions and exhortations of God's service already imply knowledge of the means of response and ability to control them; and since, in the last resort, all our responses are only forms of our actual behaviour, the knowledge of our behaviour is a necessary condition of our control of it, assuming for the moment that such control may prove to be possible. To know ourselves as we actually are—that is to say, in our current actual behaviour—may not be, and is not, the object of Religion; but it certainly forms a necessary step to Religion, and, as it would seem, the first necessary step. How can God be served if we are ignorant of the actual present behaviour of the servant? Conscious service implies self-knowledge as well as knowledge of the Being to be served. Self-consciousness or awareness of our actuality is, in short, an indispensable element in Religion as strictly defined.

How did our forefathers, who founded and practised Religion, set about attaining self-knowledge? The answer to this question would throw the first real ray of light on the nature of the religious technique. But, alas, it is not forthcoming, or forthcoming only in such dark sayings as themselves demand a key that is missing. We hear of schools where 'Mysteries' were taught, of long courses of initiation, of difficult exercises of various kinds; of Masters and pupils. And we can distinguish in the surviving text words and phrases having the air of an exact but incomprehensible connotation. How many of the words that today pass as religious had once a purely technical psychological meaning we cannot guess; but unless we are to attribute to our ancestors a mythical religious sense, it is highly probable that time alone is responsible for their present 'pious' associations. In short, if the preliminary aim of the ancient Religious Schools was the preparation of ordinary men and women for the extraordinary life of conscious co-operation with the Creator, the means employed for the necessary pre-requisite of self-knowledge must have been anything but religious in our modern sense. On the contrary, they must have been practical first and foremost; and in all probability the vocabulary of the technique was chosen from the popular science of the day.

It has been suggested that in the current theories of Behaviourism ancient Religion and Modern Science meet. Let us add, however, that they only meet, they do not as yet mingle. Nevertheless, it is in the vocabulary of Behaviourism that the technique of self-observation can best be stated; and be the outcome of the technique the re-discovery or confirmation of the ancient dogmas or their dismissal as superstitions, the new field and method of psychological research can at least be said to be promising. What, indeed, can more plainly call for rigorous self-examination than the very instruments upon which all our observations of the rest of the world depend? Behaviourists observing the behaviour of others are still at two degrees from the object nearest them; and the result is infallibly, in consequence, a closer and closer approximation to physics and ultimately to the elimination of psychology altogether. Self-observation of one's own behaviour automatically corrects this fatal error of emptying out the baby with the bath water. While observing, however objectively, my own behaviour, I am under no temptation to forget the accompanying sensations, emotions and trains of thought. I cannot overlook or under-rate the psychological element when it obtrudes itself into the very phenomena I am witnessing. And the preservation of my awareness of this concomitant of many forms of my behaviour gives a higher degree of understanding when I apply myself to the observation of others. Once this is realised, the technique of the Behaviourists may be taken straight away and applied without change to our new field. We can accept their classification of forms of behaviour, together, if necessary, with their means of measuring Man. None of their implications, even in the extreme form of organic mechanism, are positively alien to us. If self-observation be the next step in scientific Behaviourism, and it appears logically to be, the second step of Behaviourism may very well prove to be the first step in the technique of Religion.

A warning, however, is necessary. Careful and impartial observation of one's own behaviour would at the first blush appear to be as easy as the observation of the behaviour of others. Far from this, however, is the usual experience of the curious self-observer. In fact, from the very beginning of the collection of such data about one's own actual behaviour, the path is strewn with difficulties of a hitherto unrealized kind. It would almost seem that Nature resents the attempt to observe her in oneself, so powerful and at the same time so subtle is the resistance commonly experienced. Possibly it was this very discovery that led to the formulation of the dogmas of ancient Religion. They had tried to meet themselves, Nature and God, face to face!

WHAT IS THE SOUL?

THE *New Age* has lately been gently chided for using the words 'God' and the 'soul' as if they conveyed a definite meaning.

Yes, and if I could have been convinced of our error, I should have been by the argument.

Why, what was it?

That these terms have still so much superstitious theological power that for the present it is dangerous to employ them publicly. Public opinion must pass the purgatory of Atheism and Materialism before it is fit for metaphysics without theology. But my reply was that the *New Age* could not be said to be an organ of the public opinion of today, but of the public opinion of tomorrow. Our readers, in fact, have crossed the Red Sea of Materialism and the Jordan of Atheism. We can therefore safely employ the old traditional terms with a purified meaning. 'Guild' we can say without arousing the evil associations of the word, and likewise 'God' and the 'soul' are open now for us to employ without superstition.

But are the meanings attachable to these terms definite?

They are now, though, of course, they have not been for several centuries. The last person in Europe to employ the words 'God' and the 'soul' as exact terms was probably Aquinas. After him the deluge! Luther, I am convinced, had no more exact conception of what he meant by 'God' than had General Booth. Both men were secretly anthropomorphic. And these, you will observe, are the relatively classic deists: I mean that they did insist on a clear image. The remaining body of believers, on the other hand, were too sophisticated to regard God as a man, and too unmetaphysical to regard God clearly as an idea. In consequence, they swam in a fog, and saw God and the soul as bog-lights, will-o'-the-wisps, wreaths of smoke, and finally as nothing at all. For them God and the soul had ceased to have any real existence: the words were empty. But we have now returned, I think, to the possibility of definition—definition that really does define. There is nothing vague, for example, in the definition of 'God' as the 'cause of the original dispositions of matter'. You may say, if you like, that there is nothing necessarily comfortable in it, nothing essentially beneficent, nothing, in fact, traditionally associated with the theological God. On the contrary, I find in the native dispositions of matter everything, save one thing—namely, the 'soul'.

And your definitiion of the soul, if I remember, is consciousness, or that which becomes aware of the manifestation of the dispositions of matter?

Yes, that is right; but you will realize the difficulty of obtaining a clear conception of this, since we are it. The soul cannot know itself, since it cannot be both the subject and object of knowledge simultaneously. As well ask a man to stand upon his own shoulders or a bird to fly over itself as the soul to be an object of its own knowledge. The knower always remains unknown to himself.

But in that event the soul must always remain un-known!

By no means. In the first place there is a form of know-ledge which does not require a subject and an object. It is knowledge by immediacy. What we ordinarily call knowledge is the sum of our deductions from sense impressions: that is, it is derived not immediately, but mediately, through a chain of impression and deduction. But there is this other means of knowledge which dis-penses with one or more or, in the end, with *all* the intermediaries. Intuition, for example, dispenses with one of the ordinary steps; genius dispenses with two; but what the saints called illumination dispenses with all. Secondly, as we cannot look directly at the sun, but may gaze on its reflection in water, or even in the moon, so I believe, the soul is reflected in the mind, and may be intermediately and, of course, only partially known by this means. At least, it is evident that there is more in the mind than sense-impression has put there.

What, for example?

Well, without raising the controversial ghost of the origin of reason (which, by the way, I cannot regard, as the current psychologists regard it, as an evolutionary outcome of instinct), I will indicate what, in my opinion, the mind owes to the shining proximity of the soul. The desire and the hope of immortality are, of course, un-questionable. No animal entertains them. On the other hand, it has been argued that the hope of immortality which the human mind entertains is a mere balance to the human fore-knowledge of mortality, a fore-knowledge unpossessed by the animals also. But I find this immortal longing so enwoven with other qualities and powers of mind that to regard it as a mere counter-balance of our fore-knowledge of physical death is impossible. On the contrary, every noble quality which distinguishes the human race is derived from the belief in the immortality of the soul.

But even if this were the case, the truth of immortality would not be established, would it?

Agreed; but remember that what we are now seeking is a reflection in the mind of the nature of the soul. We are not asking for an intellectual conception capable of rational demonstration. From the rational point of view, the truth of immortality can only be established by the medium of sense-impressions; and since these are for the present out of the question, immortality is rationally undemonstrable. On the other hand, we have to account for the presence of the belief in the mind at all. To employ an old illustration, if a pure crystal suddenly appears scarlet, we conclude that a scarlet object has been placed near it, and has become reflected in the crystal. Similarly, if a belief appears in the mind without any sensible origin we may conclude may we not, that it is due to the contiguity of some non-sensible object? The reflection of the soul in the mind, I maintain, aroused in the latter a belief in immortality—a belief not founded on reason and not derived from sense-impressions, but a belief nevertheless.

But in many instances there is no such belief in the mind. Are we to conclude that, unless the belief in immortality exists in the mind, the soul of the man is afar off or entirely absent?

That need not necessarily be concluded, I think. Very much more may exist in the mind than is dreamt of by the articulate consciousness. The sum of our formulated beliefs may be, and usually is, far less than the sum of the beliefs on which we habitually act. In many instances, indeed, we actually deny in words what our deeds prove we hold in fact. And this accounts, perhaps, both for the noble conduct of professed atheists and materialists and the ignoble conduct of many professed believers in the immortality of the soul.

Then, actually, you do not attach much importance to belief?

Not to beliefs usually articulated. A man's verbal creed may have no real relation with the creed on which he acts. It is a very rare mind that believes what it does, and does what it actually believes. But only in such a mind are thought, feeling, and action really one.

Allowing, then, that the report of the mind is not usually to be relied upon, what evidence is there that the soul really operates on or through the mind? If the mind is not necessarily aware of it, how can anybody be aware of it?

I have said that there are the two means; the first is by immediacy, and the second is by a kind of induction. It is possible, I believe, for the soul to know itself by an act of immediacy which for the moment we may call realization. But it is also possible to discover the soul and even to learn its nature by examining its effects on the mind. We must ask ourselves what qualities exist in the mind that appear to have non-sensible origin; and, secondly, we may conclude from those qualities the nature of the power or soul that produces them there.

TALKS WITH
KATHERINE MANSFIELD
AT FONTAINEBLEAU

EVERYBODY knows that Katherine Mansfield spent her last days in the Gurdjieff Institute at Fontainebleau, and the letters and diaries which Mr. Middleton Murry has now published bear ample testimony to the value she attached both to the institute and to the system of training employed there. Many questions have been asked concerning the particular advantage other than health which Katherine Mansfield hoped to derive from it all. Had she come to the end of her writing impulse? But she was still full of sketches and plans for future stories, and even a novel or two. Was she dissatisfied with her craftsmanship, and did she hope to improve it under a special method of training? But she was always dissatisfied and always improving herself. From the age of about twenty-one, when she showed me her first sketch, and I published it in the *New Age*, to her death at thirty-three, at a moment when she was planning to write again after some month's rest, she worked, as few writers work, to develop and perfect her style in the agony of conviction that so far it was only embryonic.

Some months before she went into the institute at Fontainebleau she told me that she could not read any of the stories she had written without feeling self-contempt. 'There is not one', she said, 'that I dare show to

God'. It therefore did not need the institute to intensify her wish to excel in her craftsmanship; and, indeed, the institute was not a school of literary art, nor was she under any illusion that writing could be taught there. The real reason, and the only reason, that led Katherine Mansfield to the Gurdjieff Institute was less dissatisfaction with her craftsmanship than dissatisfaction with herself; less dissatisfaction with her stories than with the attitude toward life implied in them; less dissatisfaction with her own and contemporary literature than with literature.

I had many conversations with her on this topic during the years of our acquaintance, and particularly during the months preceding her death. She was even more explicit on these occasions than in her letters and diaries. 'Suppose', she used to say, 'that I could succeed in writing as well as Shakespeare. It would be lovely, but what then? There is something wanting in literary art even at its highest. Literature is not enough'.

'The greatest literature', she said, 'is still only mere literature if it has not a purpose commensurate with its art. Presence or absence of purpose distinguishes literature from mere literature, and the elevation of the purpose distinguishes literature within literature. That is merely literary that has no other object than to please. Minor literature has a didactic object. But the greatest literature of all—the literature that scarcely exists—has not merely an aesthetic object, nor merely a didactic object, but, in addition, a creative object: that of subjecting its readers to a real and at the same time illuminating experience. Major literature, in short, is an initiation into truth'.

'But where do we stand in relation to that?' I asked. 'Where is the writer with the keys of initiation upon him?'

This was Katherine Mansfield's introduction to the Gurdjieff Institute, and the object of her travel there. For she realized that it is not writing as writing that needs criticism, correction, and perfection, so much as the mind, character, and personality of the writer. One must become more to write better. Certainly this does not exclude the possibility of great improvement in technique without the aid of any system of personal training. On the other hand, when, as in Katherine Mansfield's case, the improvement of one's technique by the ordinary means has ceased to be possible, or has fallen under the law of diminishing returns (yielding too small a result for the effort expended), then the adoption of an entirely new means, such as special self-training, becomes imperative if the will to perfection is still as active as it was in her.

I saw Katherine Mansfield almost every day in the institute, and we had long talks together. For months she was quite content not to be writing or even reading. We had a common surprise in contrasting our current attitude towards literature with the craze we had both experienced for many years. What has come over us? she would ask whimsically. Are we dead? Or was our love of literature an affectation, which had now dropped off like a mask? Every now and then, on the other hand, a return of the old enthusiasm would be experienced. She would begin a story and confide to me that she was rather enjoying the thrill of writing again. The following day she had torn it up, quite cheerfully, and with a grimace of humour. Premature delivery! She was under contract, I believe, to write a number of stories for one publisher or another, and many times she spoke of it as an obligation. But greater even than her wish to keep her engagement with her publishers was her resolution not to write stories in the old style. Her new stories were to be different. How different only she had any real conception; and, moreover, she kept it to herself, not even confiding it to her diaries or her most intimate letters. It was, in fact, a conception to be brooded upon, and not written about—a conception that slowly arose within a new state of being and understanding; a conception, therefore, inexpressible in words until its inner metamorphoses had been completed. I read her diaries in vain for a real trace of the new idea that had begun to dawn in Katherine Mansfield. She writes in them repeatedly of new stories, but never of the new attitude to be implied and manifested in them. She would write, as before, with all her old qualities vivified and illuminated; she would continue to employ her marvellously microscopic observation of men and women. But her attitude was to have undergone a change. In a word, she would have a new purpose in writing—a purpose not only to gratify and instruct, but to initiate and create.

One day, shortly before her death, she sent for me to

come to her room; she had something very important to tell me. When I arrived, she was in high spirits. Her face shone as if she had been on Sinai.

'What is it, Katherine?' I asked. 'What makes you so happy?'

'I have found my idea', she said. 'I've got it at last. It arose, of course, out of a personal experience. Katya has felt something that she never felt before, and Katya understands something she never understood before'.

I cannot recall the exact words in which she proceeded to expound her new idea, or, rather, new attitude toward life and literature. It was, moreover, adumbrated with the aid of silences during which I thought as intensely as she on the subject; and from these she would emerge with a fresh suggestion or an improved formulation of a previous opinion. I can only record fragments, and the final impression in her mind. Briefly, the conclusion was this: to make the commonplace virtues as attractive as ordinarily the vices are made: to present the good as the witty, the adventurous, the romantic, the gay, the alluring; and the evil as the platitudinous, the dull, the conventional, the solemn, and the unattractive.

'I have not been able to think', she said, 'that I should not have made such observations as I *have* made of people, however cruel they may seem. After all, I *did* observe those things, and I had to set them down. I've been a camera. But that's just the point. I've been a selective camera, and it has been my attitude that has determined the selection; with the result that my slices of life (thank you, Mr. Phillpotts!) have been partial, misleading, and a little malicious. Further, they have had no other purpose than to record my attitude, which in itself stood in need of a change if it was to become active instead of passive. Altogether, I've been not only a mere camera, but I've been a selective camera, and a selective camera without a creative principle. And, like everything unconscious, the result has been evil'.

'Well, and what is your new plan?'

'To widen first the scope of my camera, and then to employ it for a conscious purpose—that of representing life not merely as it appears to a certain attitude, but as it appears to another and different attitude, a creative attitude'.

'What do you mean by a creative attitude?' I asked.

'You must help me out, Orage', she replied, 'if I miss the words. But I mean something like this. Life can be made to appear anything by presenting only one aspect of it; and every attitude in us—every mood, I mean to say—sees only one aspect. Assuming that this attitude is more or less permanent in any given writer, and, insusceptible of being changed by his own will, he is bound to present only the correspondent aspect of life, and, at the same time, to do no more than present it. He is passively victimised by the partial vision imposed on him, and this, in its turn, is without dynamic quality. Such reflections of life have the effect of reflections in a looking-glass of real objects; that is, none whatever'.

'Your idea is, then, to affect life and no longer just to reflect it?'

42

'Oh, that is too big', she said. 'You must not laugh at me. Help me to express myself'.

She continued with occasional suggestions of words, and finally completed the sketch of her new attitude.

'There are in life as many aspects as attitudes toward it; and aspects change with attitudes. At present we see life, generally speaking, in only a passive aspect because we bring only a passive attitude to bear upon it. Could we change our attitude, we should not only see life differently, but life itself would come to *be* different. Life would undergo a change of appearance because we ourselves had undergone a change in attitude. I'm aware, for example, of a recent change of attitude in myself: and at once not only my old stories have come to look different to me, but life itself looks different. I could not write my old stories again, or any more like them: and not because I do not see the same detail as before, but because somehow or other the pattern is different. The old details now make another pattern; and this perception of a new pattern is what I call a creative attitude towards life'.

'You mean', I said, 'that while the details of life—the forms, colours, sounds, etc.—remain the same, the pattern under which you arrange them is now different, owing to your change of attitude? Formerly, for example, being yourself in a mood, say, of resentment, you have selected and presented your observations of life in a pattern of, say, a cross of amused suffering? Your present attitude, being creative, and not, like resentment, simply reactive, arranges the same details, but in

43

a different pattern; in a pattern to present, say, the descent from the cross?'

'I wish I dare mean half as much as that', Katherine Mansfield said, 'but really my idea is much smaller. Perhaps not, though, if I come to think about it. Do you think it is very presumptuous of me?'

I reassured her, and she continued:

'An artist communicates not his vision of the world, but the attitude that results in his vision; not his dream, but his dream-state; and as his attitude is passive, negative, or indifferent, so he reinforces in his readers the corresponding state of mind. Now, most writers are merely passive; in fact, they aim only at representing life, as they say, with the consequence that their readers for the most part become even more passive, even more spectatorial, and we have a world of Peeping Toms with fewer and fewer Lady Godivas to ride by. What I am trying to say is that a new attitude to life on the part of writers would first see life different and then make it different'.

'Have you come to any practical conclusions as regards the writing of stories?' I asked. 'Do you see the possibility of a new kind of story? How will your new idea work out in practice?'

Katherine Mansfield showed me some fragments of beginnings of stories, all of which she tore up.

'I have begun many times', she said, 'but I am not yet ready, it seems. However, the idea is clear enough, and I shall carry it out one day. Here is an example. I won't say it is one I shall ever write, but it will serve as an illustration. Two people fall in love and marry. One, or perhaps both of them, have had previous affairs, the remains of which still linger like ghosts in the new home. Both wish to forget, but the ghosts still walk. How can this situation be presented? Ordinarily a writer such as the late lamented Katherine Mansfield, would bring her passive, selective, and resentful attitude to bear upon it, and the result would be one of her famous satiric sketches, reinforcing in her readers the attitude in herself. Or, peradventure, some didacticist would treat of the situation, and present us with a homily on the importance of sacrifice. Others would treat it pathetically or solemnly or psychologically or melodramatically or humorously, each according to his own passive attitude or normal mood.

'But I should represent it as my present attitude sees it, as a common adventure in ghost laying. Thanks to some change in me since I have been here, I see any such situation as an opportunity for the exercise and employment of all the intelligence, invention, imagination, bravery, endurance, and, in fact, all the virtues of the most attractive hero and heroine. Think of the subtlety necessary on both sides to maintain a mutual state of love which both naturally and sincerely wish to maintain, as, of course, everybody does. Think of how they would try to lay the ghosts in each other and in themselves. Suppose them to be jointly competing for the divine laurel and living and loving as an art. I can see such a scope for subtlety of observation that Henry James might appear myopic. At the same time, no quality need

45

necessarily remain unemployed; but every power of the artist might be brought into play'.

'You would not necessarily have a happy ending?' I asked.

'Not by any means. The problem might prove to be too big. Heroes and heroines are not measured either by what they passively endure or by what they actually achieve, but by the quantity and quality of the effort they put forth. The reader's sympathy would be maintained by the continuity and variety of the efforts of one or both of the characters, by their indomitable renewal of the struggle with ever fresh invention. Usually our "heroes" flag in their resources; they sulk after their first failure, or simply repeat the tactics which have already failed. And we are asked to admire their endurance or sympathize with their suffering or laugh at their ineptitude. I wish the laugh to be with the heroes. Let them anticipate the passive spectator and act as if the problem were theirs only to solve. That, roughly, is my new idea'.

'And you really see your way to writing stories with it?'

'I see the way, but I still have to go it'.

Only a few weeks later Katherine Mansfield was dead. I saw her a few hours before her death, and she was still radiant in her new attitude.

APHORISMS

The purpose of the Gurdjieff method is to produce men —not 'men' in quotation marks. Monstrous genius is ruled out.

Beelzebub: the actualized, ideal objective man. His function has ceased. He has a critique. He has put down his conclusions impartially, without prejudice, constructively, and hands them on to Hassein.

Sons of God: they who understand and consciously co-operate.

A normal man is one who has not only actualized his potentialities but has freed himself from his subjectivity.

A real man is one who understands why he is alive, what his body is for and what he must do.

The real man is he who can, at will, in any circumstances play the reasonable part.

Consider the 'sly' man; he tries to be aware always.

Ordinary man is at the mercy of his organism: of the instinctive centre—impressions received by the senses, of appetites, inertia, disease; of the feelings—associations connected with people and places past and present, likes and dislikes, fear and anxiety; of the mind—imagination, day-dreaming, suggestibility.

Man believes he has will: this is his illusion.

If man were truly the heir of all the ages he would be on the shoulders of his ancestors.

It has been said over and over again: Man is of the order of the moon: he collects impressions and excretes behaviour.

Man may degenerate like the ants and the bees, before he becomes extinct.

*   *   *

A being is defined in value according to the degree to which Faith, Hope and Love have become objective in him.

The gradation of beings objectively is according to their inner development. In life, people are respected for their abnormality, not for their inner development or degree of objective reason.

Being has to do with the feeling centre and depends on knowing and doing. It is the result of the struggle between the affirming and denying parts. 'A being is one who feels', and is therefore to be graded by the range and intensity of feeling. Any attempt to attain superior being directly leads to a psychopathic state.

Beings differ in the *potentiality* of their awareness.

The advantage of the terrible disadvantage of being human is to be able to be glad—whether happy or unhappy—and, by achieving consciousness, to become greater than the angels. We, becoming conscious beings, are the mind of God; angels are his emotions.

The birthright of a human being is the desire for self-consciousness, which should appear at the age of majority. At the about age of thirty there should come a sense of the world in which we live, the dawning of cosmic consciousness. After this, according to one's gifts, conditions, circumstances and so on, one should become a conscious agent in the functions of the cosmos, which is a total scheme of which we would have a relative comprehension.

To *become*, implies ascent to a higher order of being.

The universe as a conscious being is the third dimension of time.

Between the positive absolute and negative absolute—Being and Non-being—is the scale of existence, on which evolution and involution move up and down. Everything has its place on this scale: man is third from the highest, metal the lowest.

* * *

A human being is one who works with three centres; he who works with two or one is sub-human.

Every time we repress the working of a centre we become a two- or one-brained being.

We repeat in ourselves the major experiences of the planet. Two centres are struck off.

The fourth centre is a synthesis of the other three centres.

49

The universe is a being with three centres corresponding to our own.

The emotional centre is the dynamo of our whole life. In it are our wishes, which maintain us and our bodies in life. Wishes are on different planes. The highest wish, once felt, never can be displaced.

Neurotic syptoms are due to the three centres being out of step with each other, out of harmony—one centre being in a definitely different tempo and intensity from the others.

★   ★   ★

Objective Reason is that which is immortal. The effort I make to become objective transforms substances which thereby become permanent, immortal. I acquire a permanent 'I' which is independent of the vicissitudes of life, aware of a conscious purpose, which persists through ups and downs, through runs of good and bad luck.

Reason is the sum of the normal functions of a human being—not ordinary logical reasoning or ratiocination.

Reason is developed by going against habits and repetition; by following a legitimate whim; by not doing as others do.

Pondering is answering questions from essence and answering them practically. One-third of one's time should be spent in pondering.

Pondering is intellectual assimilation.

Pondering implies the use of both mind and emotion.

Pondering is proper only to a being.

Contemplation is contact with thought-forms left by other beings interested in objective reason.

The world of ideas is populated as is the world of nature. The ability to treat ideas as if they were things, to distinguish between them, would be objective thought.

No statement can be understood without the effort of conscious assimilation: this brings realization.

Realization: when that which is known is also felt and sensed.

Controlled imagination becomes mental work.

Introspection is a form of lunacy.

It is impossible for us to arrive at a judgement of ourselves through introspection—this judgement is sociologically conditioned.

Reasoning is the locomotion of the thinking centre, which is composed of definite organs—concentration, pondering, meditation, contemplation. Logical progression is the ordinary locomotion of the thinking centre as a whole. Life in the planetary body is sensation; in the astral body, emotion; in the mental body, thought.

Instinctive reason we share with the animals but have a higher type of it; associative reason functions according to verbal associations; of objective reason we know practically nothing—it can be acquired only by Voluntary Conscious Labour and Intentional Suffering.

The reason of ordinary man is the reason of knowledge. The reason of normal man is the reason of understanding. Knowledge is temporary, can be changed. Understanding is permanent—unchangeable.

Osiris is a wish to understand cut into fragments. Our task is to integrate our real wishes. This is at-one-ment.

The mind is a dragon which will not answer questions clearly. It must be slain, by making it answer clearly.

We do not act reasonably according to our reason.

Mere intellectualism, mere philosophy, produces monsters.

★ ★ ★

Atlantis: the submerged objective conscience swallowed up in personality. Voluntary Conscious Labour and Intentional Suffering disinter the buried conscience.

Objective conscience is the function of a normal being; the representative of God in the essence. Buried so deeply that it remains relatively indestructible.

John the Baptist: Objective conscience crying in the wilderness of the body. Conscience beheaded by external life. 'Behold the Lamb of God'—the 'I'.

God is the 'I' of the universe.

Krishna: the 'I' of Arjuna.

It is said: If thine 'I' be single thy whole body shall be full of light. 'I' and the Father are one. Be still, and know that 'I' am God.

The 'bridge' in ancient religions meant the Way—the Way of Buddha, the Way of Jesus. 'I' am the Way, meaning not himself but whatever you call 'I'.

There is an 'I', a potential soul. If we can say with the same simplicity 'I have a body' as we say 'I have a car' we can begin to realize that this body is a transforming machine which 'I' can have. 'I' have a machine to use, does not mean 'I' am a machine. 'I' have a body, a mechanical organism whose function it is to transform substances and energies.

'I' is the moral agent; objective morality proceeds from 'I'.

'I' is the Messiah, for whom the creature is waiting.

*   *   *

Religion is the study and practice of perfection and it is summed up in the text: 'Be ye perfect, even as your Father in Heaven is perfect'.

Buddha, Pythagoras, Jesus Christ, were practical workmen.

Religion is a means for expanding being, for enlarging consciousness. *Religions* may confine expansion to one centre.

Religiousness is an emotional attitude to the question: 'Why was I born'.

Prayer is wish in three centres, plus effort in three centres.

God is good, and He wishes a fulfilment for beings in the universe that they also may enjoy bliss and become Sons —that they may enter into the psychology of the Being who created theWorld.

God has shared with us his suffering that we might also share in his creation.

God's wish to live is shared by all beings.

God has a purpose and it is the function of normal beings to try to comprehend that purpose.

Literally we are living in the body of God.We are made in the image of God : God's fancy is immortality.

To become self-conscious in our highest part is to become a part of God.

God is the psyche of the universe.

In us the psyche is the field of activity plus the form of the field. Within the field are three centres—God the Father, God the Son, and God the Holy Ghost.

*　　*　　*

Consciousness is an electrical phenomenon which arises from a state of being which we can feel.

Unless we can 'remember' ourselves, we are completly mechanical. Self-observation is possible only through self-remembering. These are the first steps in self-consciousness.

Conscious Faith, Hope and Love are the growing ends of essence. Faith is confidence, not mere belief. Hope is effort, not wish; effort to make it so; not a wish that it may be so.

Belief is a luxury—only those who have real knowledge have a right to believe; otherwise belief is merely plausible opinion.

Voluntary Conscious Labour: that which is made against the inertia and mechanism of the organism; not for personal gain or profit, exercise, health, sport, pleasure, or science; not out of pique, or like or dislike.

With conscious work individuality takes the place of personality. Individuality grows from essence.

You can learn to know when you are making effort consciously by your experience of making effort physically, by overcoming inner inertia—pushing against the collar.

Individuality is the consciousness of Will.

*　　*　　*

Time is a perpetual perishing. It is the enemy of God.

Time is the most important thing next to awareness. The flow of time through us gives us an opportunity to extract what we can. Time is the three-fold stream flowing through our three centres. We fish in time's 'ever-rolling' stream; what we catch is ours, but what we don't is gone. Time does not wait for us to catch everything in the stream, but if we catch enough we shall have enough to form the higher bodies—and thereby become enduring.

Time is the sum of our potential experiences, the totality of our possible experiences. We live our experiences successively; this is the first dimension of time.

To be able to live experiences simultaneously is adding another or second dimension to Time. To be aware of this simultaneity is called solid Time, or the third dimension of Time. When we have identified ourselves with Time it shall be as in Revelations: 'And there shall be Time no longer'.

Just at that moment of Time when we can say: 'The thing that is happening to me', will we be safe.

Gurdjieff says: 'Time is the Unique Subjective'.

* * *

Nature, from one aspect, is the wicked step-mother of the fairy tales, beguiling us and using us for her own purposes—the evolution of substances.

A flock of sheep exists for the objective purpose of providing mutton and wool. Perhaps we can cheat our fate in this, although we shall then serve another objective purpose.

The black sheep finds itself very odd among the others. Our interest lies in the individual—the rebel with an inkling. Speaking of sheep, ponder over the nursery rhyme: 'Black sheep, black sheep, have you any wool? Yes sir, yes sir, three bags full. One for the master, one for the dame, one for the little boy that lives down the lane'. And the other one: 'Little boy blue, come blow up your horn . . . he's under a haycock fast asleep'.

Nature is genius without common sense.

Nature is the objective creditor of every living being.

★   ★   ★

Scientists are engaged in anatomizing the corpse of the universe.

Ordinary scientist: one who possesses an assortment of information not verified by personal experience, and which is often disproved by another 'scientist'.

Science sees everything mechanically, through part of the moving-instinctive centre. It has no answer to human needs in a crisis.

Science is occupied with 'how', not 'why'.

To discover not more and more things but the truth or real relation of things is what distinguishes men from the animals.

Ordinary knowledge is awareness of external facts; ordinary belief, conviction on inadequate grounds.

Objective Science is that which has as its conscious purpose the investigating of the meaning and aim of existence.

★   ★   ★

The universe is the body of God. It is the neutralizing force of the Sun Absolute; the manifestation of the struggle between the positive and the negative forces of God.

57

Planets are enormous beings and have relations among themselves as do people. They have their likes and dislikes, their tensions; they are sympathetic or antipathetic to each other.

Our world, the earth, is the note mi in one of the cosmic rays: the localization in space of two thousand million distorted beings—the lunatic planet.

* * *

To know ourselves is to know the universe.

Speaking of self-knowing it is said in the uncanonical gospels: 'The Kingdom of God is within you. Seek therefore to know yourselves and you shall know that you are the city and that you are in the city'. 'Follow me and you shall lose me; follow yourselves and you shall find both me and yourselves'.

Discover 'chief feature', never mind where it comes from. Non-identify with it and it will no longer trouble you.

The observation of others is coloured by our inability to observe ourselves impartially. We can never be impartial about anything until we can be impartial about our own organism.

* * *

We are primarily concerned with ourselves as judging agents; and the proper study of every individual is himself or herself. Only he who has attempted to judge himself can have an idea of judging anyone else. An aphorism in the Study House at the Prieuré says: 'Judge others by yourself and you will rarely be mistaken.'

Our fulfilment is imposed on us. This may be called justice.

Objective art produces a state of non-identification. It is concerned with inner development.

True artists are the antennae of nature. Coming nature casts its artists before it. The Bohemian is the typical subjective artist, expressing himself.

Pursue art, pursue reason.

It is possible to have aesthetic emotions and to be without human emotions.

There is no such thing as an immortal work of art. There is one art—the greatest of all, the art of making a complete human being of oneself.

* * *

Essence is a chemical deposit from the sun and planets of the solar system, which enters earth-beings at the moment of conception. In man this affects the region of the solar plexus. It is unlike any of the chemicals found on this planet, and links man to the cosmos. As the chemicals of the physical body return to this planet after death so do the chemicals of essence return to their sources.

Truth before God is essence; 'truth' before man is personality.

Will: only that which is self-initiated, not obliged, not wanted by the organism. An effort to accomplish an 'I' wish, not 'it' wish.

Remorse: sorrow for not having acted according to objective conscience.

Pity is divine; self-pity diabolical.

Redemption is the ultimate actualization of potentialities—to 'be what we must be'.

Voluntary, or intentional, suffering is the price of immortality.

Honest doubt is suspended judgment.

Commonsense mellowed and experienced is wisdom; and wisdom in its ripeness is beauty.

Anger and hatred are negative emotions only when they are misdirected. Never fear to hate the odious.

Humour: a form of intuition.

Intuition with certainty is judgment.

Egoism: measuring others by our likes and dislikes—not by their needs but by our preferences.

Vanity: that something for which we will sacrifice almost anything rather that that it should be hurt.

Pride: ignorant presumption that the qualities and status of the organism are due to merit.

Superstition: an emotional attitude towards a lie.

Sentimentality: a slight emotion exaggerated by muddled thinking. 'Do noble deeds, and regret them all day long'.

Wit: a form of sex display.

Would you see the devil? Look in the mirror.

Be a pianist, not a piano.

The happy person is he who is striving to actualize his potentialities.

There is little difference in the experiences of different people—the difference consists in what they do with them. The importance of our first food is not so much in the quantity and quality as in the digesting of it. Experiences are another form of food; from this point of view it does not matter much what happens as how we take experiences.

Life should be a voluntary overcoming of difficulties, those met with and those voluntarily created, otherwise it is just a dice-game.

We should strive to do more and more, better and better, and think less and less about it.

Nothing I can do, even if I do my best, can be *good*. As Jesus said, 'We are unprofitable servants, we have done our duty'. Therefore I shall strive to do my best.

Don't play with algebra when you have not studied arithmetic. 'Seek ye first the Kingdom of Heaven'. Be as a little child—concerned with himself.

Feel with the brain, think with the heart, act practically.

Formulate your feelings as well as your thoughts.

Whatever involves mental, emotional or physical waste we call immoral.

There is a complete protection available to you—silence.

Psychological exercises are for the purpose of obtaining freedom of movement for the astral and mental bodies. Begin by teaching them to crawl.

Beware of premature exercises.

Conditional immortality is to be contrasted with the impossible immortality of Tennyson — those who 'faintly trust the larger hope'. 'Immortality entails responsibility'.

There must be *something* to explain why we are all such fools; why we are not self-conscious; why we treat ourselves with such care. There is something: it is Kundabuffer.

The realization of ignorance is the beginning of wisdom.

There is more joy in Heaven over one perfected man than in ninety-nine naturally evolved angels.

The last degree of esoteric teaching is plain common sense.

I beg you before starting on this journey
to question—you are plunging into
the dark. Here is a little lamp;
I show you how to rub it;
make sure you know
how to rub
it

ALFRED RICHARD ORAGE *was born of a poor family in Yorkshire in January* 1873. *A few months later his parents returned to his father's native place in Huntingdonshire. Here Orage went to the village school, and would have gone to work at the age of twelve had not the local squire, impressed with his intelligence and charm, made it possible for him to continue his studies, and eventually go to a teachers' training college. He was twenty-one when he obtained a post at the Leeds Board School, and for the next ten years earned his living by teaching children of various ages, beginning with the youngest.*

This, he claimed, was an excellent preparation for his later teaching of adults. In the true sense an educator, he was able to draw people out and get them to formulate their thoughts and feelings. He had, in a high degree, the rare quality of emotional understanding, together with a gaiety and a sense of humour. Not long after coming to Leeds he met a kindred spirit in Holbrook Jackson, and the two young men formed groups to study the philosophers, and, later, they started the Leeds Arts Club, which soon became a sensational success. In the meantime Orage developed his talent for public speaking in the open air as well as at meetings with Socialists and Theosophists; he also did a good deal of work as a member of the Society for Psychical Research. Throughout his activities in these varied fields, and with the Nietzscheans, Platonists and Fabians, his heart of fire was tempered with a brain of ice which prevented his being caught up in the sentimentality which so often surrounds such groups; he taught with a critical mind that questioned everything.

At the age of thirty he gave up school-teaching and went to London. He became a journalist, and for the first year made hardly enough to exist on. Holbrook Jackson had also gone to London, forsaking the lace trade for journalism. Hearing that 'The New Age' was for sale Jackson and Orage decided to acquire it, and induced a number of people, Bernard Shaw among them, to put up the necessary money. They soon discovered that a 'views-paper', a paper of ideas, can never pay its way. Jackson left to become a successful publisher and a noted bibliophile, while Orage remained to become, according to his contemporaries, the most brilliant editor that England had had for a hundred years. Almost everyone of note in the world of arts and letters—among them, Chesterton, Arnold Bennett, Belloc, Shaw and Wells—wrote for the paper, and most of them for nothing. In its columns friends were criticized impartially as were foes. It was also a school of literature with Orage as a sort of elder brother critic which produced more than forty young writers who made their name. What many felt is expressed in a letter to him from Katherine Mansfield. She said: 'I want to thank you for all you let me learn from you. I am still very low down in the school. But you taught me to write, you taught me to think; you showed me what was to be done and what not to do. . . But let me thank you, Orage. Thank you for everything. . . .

> Yours in admiration and gratitude,
> Katherine Mansfield.'

For fourteen years Orage continued to edit 'The New Age'. His reputation as a literary critic and writer on current affairs in almost every field of human effort was at its height when an inner discontent began increasingly to manifest itself. With all his searching he had not been able to find an answer to the question which never allowed him to sleep in peace—the question of the meaning and aim of existence. The possibility of finding an answer, however, was nearer than he supposed. P. D. Ouspensky, whom he had been in touch with for some time, arrived in London in the Autumn of 1921 and spoke with him about the teachings of G. I. Gurdjieff. Orage, with Rowland Kenney, organised a study group for Ouspensky which first met at the studio of the late Lady Rothermere in Circus Road, N.W. After some months of work Gurdjieff himself visited the group in London. His talks convinced Orage that he had found the teacher he was looking for, a teacher who had, as well as a system of ideas, a practical method for inner development, a method by which he would have the possibility of being able to discover and understand the answers to his questions. This realization led him to make a complete break with his old life; and, in October 1922, to the bewilderment of many, he sold 'The New Age', gave up his brilliant life in London—the talks in Chancery Lane, conversations in the Café Royal, public affairs, Ouspensky's groups—and went to live in the Gurdjieff Institute at the Chateau du Prieuré in Fontainebleau.

A year later, in December 1923, he went to New York as Gurdjieff's representative—the latter arriving a week later with his pupils to give a number of demonstrations of sacred dances and movements of the East. Before Gurdjieff returned to France he asked Orage to settle in New York and teach his ideas. Thus began a new and full life for Orage; and for seven years, apart from visits to the Prieuré, he remained in America working for Gurdjieff. One of his accepted tasks, for him very difficult, was to raise money for a fund to enable Gurdjieff to write his book 'All and Everything: An Objectively Impartial Criticism of the Life of Man; or, Beelzebub's Tales to His Grandson'. For some twenty years the greater part of the contribution to this fund came from the American groups. Another of Orage's tasks was to put the book ('Beelzebub' as it was then called) into readable English. Although he worked for several years on the book he did not live to finish the revision.

The following letter gives an eloquent portrait of Orage during his last years in America. It is from John Cowper Powys, author of many books.

1930.

Route 2, Hillsdale, N.Y.

Dear Orage,

Neither my friend P. nor I can get you out of our heads. We have agreed that your visit to us was the greatest event of our winter in Patchin Place. We came to the conclusion that whatever ambiguousness there may be in the nature of your mythology there must be something profoundly right in your own attitude towards it. There's something so 'fixed-up', so unctuous and conceited about these Indian Swamis and esoteric teachers, just as there is about Christian Scientists, something that is unilluminating and does not vibrate to the shocks of real life, something that seems to face life through wads of cotton-wool. We go on puzzling ourselves as to exactly what it is that makes your philosophy so different from this; what it is that makes your philosophy so fresh and natural and faltering and troubled as all genuine attitudes to life ought to be, tenuous and almost brittle and with a peculiar sort of humility in it—no! not exactly brittle; but shaky and troubled and insecure—like Nietzsche and Unamuno and Pascal and Heraclitus. The impression you left was what Spengler calls Magian—like something Early Christian or like those early heretics. We got so strongly the feeling that however unsatisfactory and even to be condemned your gods might be, your attitude towards them was curiously right and full of incidental illumination like that of Jesus to Jehovah. Whatever cult of consciousness yours may be, its effect on your hearers is startling to people as clairvoyant in certain directions as my friend P. and I are. You are undoubtedly right in making so much of humility. That organon of research, that plummet into salt seas, that wise serpent-belly, that Taoistic

67

water seeking its level, has not only been neglected by Greeks and Romans but completely neglected, or indeed not known or heard of, by the stupid thick-skinned bastard-idealists of our time. We got the impression of actually and really—don't be angry now!—having entertained a real Saint that day. It was a very queer feeling. As if you had been a person in armour but who was secretly bleeding from wounds invisible. You didn't convert us one inch or one-hundredth part of an inch to your particular gods or ritual or doctrines or master— But you compelled us and still compel us to accept yourself in your present mood as possessed of some extraordinary psychic secret (one great portion of which is this transcendental humility or whatever it may be).

I think we both snatched at some drop of this virtue or aura or emanation and have used it ever since as a test of spiritual values. It is extraordinary. You alone of all men of genius I have ever met seem totally to have conquered pride. And when one thinks how silly such pride has made people; and how it has spoilt their art—like Victor Hugo, like D'Annunzio, like Tolstoy, it seems to me a triumph of true Machiavellianism of the spirit to have burrowed below this great block of Portland cement into wonderful interstices of moon-agate and moonstone below.

But I do think the whole thing is in the Daimonic saintliness which you have somehow, by some extraordinary trick, appropriated to yourself. Those 'secrets' you speak of that you would be willing to follow the Devil Himself in order to learn—we must confess—my friend P. and I—to regard as of slight importance compared with this magical effect which 'the humility of the hunt' after them has produced in you and which is, in itself, so we allow ourselves to feel, a kind of Absolute and something infinitely superior to any force that started you on such a path or to any tangible 'secrets' that such a path can lead to. It's no good your telling me that

68

Jesus thought Jehovah was as 'good' as He was Himself. We know what Jehovah was better than Jesus! But of course if for Jehovah you put Life, it is true that any man of exceptional genius like yourself comes much closer to Life by keeping his skin naked so to say (naked in humility) than by twining it round with those flannel swaddling bands Augustus, according to Suetonius, used; or even by wearing the proud armour of Lucifer. This is a woman's letter, my good lord, as well as a man's, so this particular tone (of handing out bouquets); almost 'maternal'; which would be intolerably impertinent from a lecturer to so formidable a literary and philosophical critic—is natural and harmless (and not impertinent at all or cool or cheeky) in two of us uniting our wits. Indeed I guess it will always take the double wit, of a man and a woman combined, to deal with so subtle a Demonic Saint as yourself! What we secretly feel ourselves is that you will eventually reach a point when you have attained the extreme of humility such as no longer to be in the least danger of Luciferan pride—and at that point we hold the view . . . Well—let that go. . . . We know nothing really about it. But sometimes out of the mouths of clumsy onlookers—you know? —even a sage can get something. . . . At any rate you certainly made us both think a lot, and as for anything 'fantastic' about it all—we are completly with you there. In the 'fantastic' lies the essence of things.

Well—I must stop. If in the future you not only defy but separate yourself from all outward authority but that of the Daimon in your own being it will only be, I fancy, when this planetary humility of yours that has proved so illuminating has gone the full length of its serpent's tail! And this may not be far off.—Life is more than any authority. They are all stepping-stones and jumping-off places.

Well—good luck go with Orage, you certainly won not only our hero-worship but our most anxious love on your behalf, but that must be a common experience to you in your strange passage through the world.

Good luck to you,

John Cowper Powys.

Towards the end of his seventh year in America he decided that the time had come for him to go back to England and put into practice what he had learnt from Gurdjieff. He afterwards said that in many ways this period in America had been one of the most satisfying of his life. From his teacher's exacting discipline and the congenial work with the groups in New York there emerged a humbler, bigger, more under-standing, and a more youthful man. He returned to England for good in 1931, and in April of 1932 brought out the first number of 'The New English Weekly'. According to Mr. T. S. Eliot, Orage at this time was the best leader writer and finest literary critic of his day. He was also the most pene-trating writer on economics. The paper became a centre of gravity for those who were studying the causes of the disas-trous breakdown of the financial system. It seemed that the paper had appeared in the midst of this economic chaos for a specific purpose. Orage's office in Cursitor Street was the scene of constant talks and meetings. Towards the end of the paper's third year this purpose appeared to have been accom-plished. During all this time Orage had neither taught Gurdjieff's ideas nor talked much about them, except to those of us who had been with him at the Prieurié; and he never again saw Ouspensky. But now he began to make fresh plans. D. Mitrinovic, who was interested in Gurdjieff's ideas, was bringing out a new magazine, and Orage had arranged to be co-editor with him. Orage also intended to introduce some of Gurdjieff's ideas into the pages of 'The New English Weekly', and to take up work with him again. We were discussing these matters during our usual walk up Chancery Lane on the way home—it was the end of October 1934. Then the talk came round to our life at Fontainebleau and our friends in New York. Suddenly he turned to me and said, 'You know, I thank God every day of my life that I met Gurdjieff'. A week later he was dead.

Gurdjieff once said, 'I loved Orage as a brother'. There was indeed in him, together with the inevitable human faults and weaknesses—the denying part—such a composition of the positive qualities that all sorts and conditions of men could not help but love and respect him.

His body lies in Old Hampstead Churchyard. On the stone is the enneagram carved by his friend Eric Gill, with Krishna's words to Arjuna: 'You grieve for those that should not be grieved for. The wise grieve neither for the living nor the dead. Never at any time was I not, nor thou, nor these princes of men. Nor shall we ever cease to be hereafter. The unreal has no being. The real never ceases to be'.

S. C. NOTT.

The four essays in this book were written after he came in contact with the Gurdjieff system of ideas. Of the aphorisms, almost all of them were given out in his talks to the groups in New York 1924-30.

Other writings of

A. R. Orage

Friedrich Nietzsche, the Dionysian Spirit of the Age	1906
Nietzsche in Outline and Aphorism	1907
Consciousness: Animal, Human and Superman	1907
An ABC of Economics	1917
Readers and Writers	1920
The Active Mind, 15 Psychological Essays	1929
The Art of Reading	1930
Psychological Exercises	1930
The BBC Speech. Together with The Age of Leisure	1934
Selected Economic Writings,	1934
Selected Essays, edited by Herbert Read and Denis Saurat	1935